I0021973

The EU Data Protection Code of Conduct for Cloud Service Providers

A guide to compliance

The EU Data Protection Code of Conduct for Cloud Service Providers

A guide to compliance

ALAN CALDER

IT Governance Publishing

Every possible effort has been made to ensure that the information contained in this book is accurate at the time of going to press, and the publisher and the author cannot accept responsibility for any errors or omissions, however caused. Any opinions expressed in this book are those of the author, not the publisher. Websites identified are for reference only, not endorsement, and any website visits are at the reader's own risk. No responsibility for loss or damage occasioned to any person acting, or refraining from action, as a result of the material in this publication can be accepted by the publisher or the author.

Apart from any fair dealing for the purposes of research or private study, or criticism or review, as permitted under the Copyright, Designs and Patents Act 1988, this publication may only be reproduced, stored or transmitted, in any form, or by any means, with the prior permission in writing of the publisher or, in the case of reprographic reproduction, in accordance with the terms of licences issued by the Copyright Licensing Agency. Enquiries concerning reproduction outside those terms should be sent to the publisher at the following address:

IT Governance Publishing Ltd
Unit 3, Clive Court
Bartholomew's Walk
Cambridgeshire Business Park
Ely, Cambridgeshire
CB7 4EA
United Kingdom
www.itgovernancepublishing.co.uk

© Alan Calder 2021

The author has asserted the rights of the author under the Copyright, Designs and Patents Act, 1988, to be identified as the author of this work.

First published in the United Kingdom in 2021 by IT Governance Publishing.

ISBN 978-1-78778-342-3

ABOUT THE AUTHOR

Alan Calder founded IT Governance Limited in 2002 and began working full time for the company in 2007. He is now Group CEO of GRC International Group plc, the AIM-listed company that owns IT Governance Ltd. Prior to this, Alan had a number of roles including CEO of Business Link London City Partners from 1995 to 1998 (a government agency focused on helping growing businesses to develop), CEO of Focus Central London from 1998 to 2001 (a training and enterprise council), CEO of Wide Learning from 2001 to 2003 (a supplier of e-learning) and the Outsourced Training Company (2005). Alan was also chairman of CEME (a public private sector skills partnership) from 2006 to 2011.

Alan is an acknowledged international cyber security guru and a leading author on information security and IT governance issues. He has been involved in the development of a wide range of information security management training courses that have been accredited by the International Board for IT Governance Qualifications (IBITGQ). Alan has consulted for clients in the UK and abroad, and is a regular media commentator and speaker.

For information about Alan's other publications, visit:

www.itgovernancepublishing.co.uk/author/alan-calder.

CONTENTS

Contents

INTRODUCTION

The introduction of the EU General Data Protection Regulation (GDPR) in 2018 marked a significant shift in how organisations process and protect personal data. Stringent new requirements, coupled with the very real threat of large financial penalties and reputational damage, forced organisations to adapt.

Article 40 of the GDPR explicitly encourages the development of codes of conduct and certifications that organisations can use to demonstrate compliance with the Regulation. Although work had already started on several such codes when the GDPR took effect, development and approval is a slow process involving many stakeholders, so organisations had little choice but to forge their own path to compliance – often using established, internationally recognised standards such as ISO 27001.

Formally founded in 2017, the EU Data Protection Code of Conduct for Cloud Service Providers (otherwise known as the EU Cloud Code of Conduct; the Code) is a voluntary code of conduct created specifically to support GDPR compliance within the business-to-business (B2B) Cloud industry. The EU Commission, the Article 29 Working Party (now the European Data Protection Board (EDPB)), the EU Directorate-General for Justice and Consumers, and Cloud-industry leaders have all contributed to its development, resulting in a robust framework that recognises the unique requirements of the Cloud industry.

The Belgian supervisory authority issued a draft decision on the suitability of the Code in February 2021 and requested the opinion of the EDPB in line with the requirements of the GDPR.

The EDPB's opinion approving the Code was published in May 2021, formally permitting its use by in-scope organisations.[1]

This pocket guide is intended to help you understand and implement the Code within your organisation.

Why should my organisation use the Code?

Compliance with the GDPR requires more than just box-ticking. Organisations must meet an array of technical and organisational requirements that extend beyond information security into privacy and governance, and the Cloud industry in particular must ensure that its services – which by design involve accessing and transferring data across the Internet, exposing it to far greater risk than data stored and processed within an organisation's internal network – meet or exceed the GDPR's requirements in order to provide the security and privacy that the market expects.

The GDPR also obligates data controllers to only use data processors that can provide "sufficient guarantees to implement technical and organisational measures in such a manner that processing will meet the requirements of this Regulation and ensure the protection of the rights of the data subject" (Article 28). Adherence to an Article 40 Code of Conduct is one way of meeting this requirement, and the EU Cloud Code of Conduct is a comprehensive and adaptable example of such a code.

Scope and structure of the Code

The Code is intended for use by B2B Cloud services where the service provider acts as a data processor (including sub-

---

[1] European Data Protection Board, *Opinion 16/2021 on the draft decision of the Belgian Supervisory Authority regarding the "EU Data Protection Code of Conduct for Cloud Service Providers" submitted by Scope Europe*, May 2021, *https://edpb.europa.eu/system/files/2021-05/edpb_opinion_202116_eucloudcode_en.pdf*.

processors). It does not apply to business-to-consumer (B2C) Cloud services or to any processing in which the service provider acts as a data controller. Additionally, the Code cannot be used to demonstrate the lawfulness of international transfers.

The Code is available to Cloud service providers throughout the European Economic Area (EEA). At the time of writing, the Code has not been approved by the UK Information Commissioner's Office (ICO) for use under the UK GDPR.

The requirements of the Code are structured into two sections:

1. "Data Protection"
2. "Security Requirements"

Each section contains specific requirements that must be met to achieve compliance (signified by 'shall' or 'must'), supported by implementation advice (signified by 'may', 'should' and 'can').

The principal requirements of the Code are referred to as 'controls'. To aid implementation, the Code contains an annex (the 'Controls Catalogue') that maps each control against the relevant GDPR requirement and equivalent controls in related international standards and frameworks, including ISO 27001, NIST SP 800-53 and SOC 2. However, there are mandatory requirements (statements that say the organisation 'shall' or 'must' do something) within the body of the Code that are not directly represented within the catalogue, so organisations cannot base their implementation project on the catalogue alone.

ISO 27001 – the international standard for information security management systems (ISMSs) – is particularly relevant to organisations that wish to comply with the Code. Control 6.1.C of the Code requires organisations to implement an ISMS in accordance with the requirements of ISO 27001 or an equivalent international standard. As the majority of the Code's data protection controls and all the security controls are linked to requirements in ISO 27001, organisations that are developing an ISMS for the first time would be well-advised to use ISO 27001 over the alternatives and thereby avoid the need to spend additional time justifying alternative controls as equivalent to those in the Code. Those that already operate a formal ISMS in line with the requirements of other standards are unlikely to find a move to ISO 27001 cost-effective or appropriate, but their greater familiarity with the underlying principles on which an ISMS is founded should make demonstrating equivalence relatively painless.

Implementing an ISMS is no small undertaking. Most organisations do so with the intent of achieving independent certification, whether to win new contracts that mandate a certified ISMS as a condition of entry to the tender process, or to reassure clients and partners of their commitment to information security in a more formal manner.

Certification inevitably comes with a price tag, albeit one that generally scales with the size of the organisation and the consequent scope of the ISMS. Recognising the burden this may place on smaller organisations, the guidance for control 6.1.C is explicit that certification of the ISMS is not required to achieve certification under the Code. Organisations should note, however, that of the three possible levels of certification offered by the Code, levels two and three cannot be achieved without independent, third-party certificates and audits of the sort that would naturally arise from a certified ISMS.

The remaining sections of the Code define the assessment and monitoring framework and the internal governance of the Code and its related organisations. Assessment and monitoring are the responsibility of SCOPE Europe, an organisation appointed by the Belgian supervisory authority as monitoring body.[2]

---

[2] For more information, visit: *https://scope-europe.eu/en/projects/eu-cloud-code-of-conduct/*.

CHAPTER 1: DATA PROTECTION REQUIREMENTS

This chapter deals primarily with the organisational aspects of information security and compliance with the GDPR. Taken as a whole, it requires strict oversight of the contents of Cloud services agreements and the development of procedures to ensure lawful processing. During implementation, the organisation should consider listing all such requirements and procedures in a single spreadsheet or document to use as a gap analysis that will support the project.

5.1 Terms and conditions of the Cloud services agreement

Contracts and agreements play a key role in the provision of Cloud services and special care must be taken to ensure they meet all requirements. While existing Cloud services agreements should already meet the requirements of the GDPR, the organisation will need to review them to ensure they also meet the requirements of the Code.

The Code stipulates that contracts and agreements for the relevant Cloud services must meet all requirements of the GDPR, particularly those contained in Article 28(3) regarding the contractual obligations of the data processor (Code 5.1.A), and that they must provide for similar but no less protective data protection obligations as those defined in the Code (5.1.B).

Agreements must define, document and assign responsibilities for both the organisation and the customer with respect to the security measures required by Article 32 of the GDPR (5.1.C). These should be agreed between parties at a level of detail sufficient to ensure legal clarity in the event of a dispute, and should reference specific technical and organisational measures (information security controls, procedures, records, etc.) and the roles responsible for them.

The organisation is expected to have established, documented procedures that ensure its employees are aware of the Code, its requirements and the need to comply, so that the provider can deal with any queries raised by the customer in an effective manner (5.1.D). Existing training and awareness procedures could be adapted to meet this requirement, though organisations that do not have formal training and awareness procedures should note that 'established' implies a mature procedure that has been in operation for some time, not one developed and implemented a few days before certification. 5.1.E of the Code requires the organisation to inform customers of its adherence to the Code in line with the requirements for use of compliance marks (etc.) defined in part 7.6.4.

The agreement must define the terms under which the organisation processes personal data on the customer's behalf (5.1.F), including subject matter and duration, types of personal data, categories of data subjects, and the obligations and rights of the controller. It must also define the conditions under which sub-processors may be engaged (5.1.G), and the processing activities the organisation and any sub-processors will perform in relation to the customer's personal data (5.1.H). These components should be part of any GDPR-compliant Cloud services agreement between data controllers and data processors, and any absence evident on review of the organisation's agreements should provoke a separate investigation into the mechanisms used to ensure legal compliance.

5.2 Processing personal data lawfully

Part 5.2 deals with the lawfulness of processing under the GDPR. The organisation must help the customer to comply with relevant obligations under Article 28 (5.2.A) and must establish documented procedures defining how the customer can access the information necessary to meet those obligations (5.2.B). The organisation must inform the customer about these procedures and the mechanisms made available to access the information (5.2.C). In line with Article 28(3)(a) of the GDPR, the organisation may only process the customer's personal data in accordance with the customer's instructions, the scope of which must be defined in the Cloud services agreement (5.2.D).

This part also requires the organisation to develop and implement data retention policies and schedules, and the procedures to maintain them, that ensure the customer's data is not retained or otherwise processed for longer than is necessary (5.2.E). These should define the duration for which customer data is retained after a Cloud services agreement is terminated, to enable response to information security or data protection incidents, to respond to investigations by supervisory authorities, and any legally mandated retention periods that may apply to specific categories of data.

Employees must be trained on the organisation's retention policies and schedules, and appropriate monitoring mechanisms must be implemented to ensure that the schedules are adhered to (5.2.F). Such mechanisms might include internal audits, automated logging, periodic reviews, or other suitable methods. Deficiencies identified through monitoring should be resolved at the earliest opportunity, ideally through a corrective action or continual improvement procedure.

The last requirement of this part obligates the organisation to communicate information about its standard retention schedules and policies to customers (5.2.G). This can be achieved by making the information available on a website, in the Cloud services agreement, or through accompanying materials provided during the sales process.

5.3 Sub-processing

In line with Article 28 of the GDPR, data processors may not engage sub-processors without prior authorisation by the data controller. This part obligates the organisation to obtain the customer's written authorisation before engaging sub-processors (5.3.A), and to follow processes agreed in the Cloud services agreement in the event the customer rejects the proposed sub-processor (5.3.B). The organisation must provide alternative options if this occurs, either by proposing alternative sub-processors or allowing the customer to terminate the contract, and it must develop a mechanism through which customers are notified of any addition or replacement of sub-processors before any data is transmitted or processed (5.3.F).

The organisation must also establish documented processes that ensure sub-processors are only engaged if they provide appropriate guarantees of GDPR compliance (5.3.C), and that the necessary technical and organisational measures are in place to ensure a level of data protection and security at least equal to those agreed between the organisation and the customer (5.3.D). These measures must apply across the entire sub-processing chain and should be clearly defined in all relevant contracts or agreements. The organisation is liable to the customer for any data protection failure on behalf of engaged sub-processors, so it is critical that the processes developed to ensure data protection and security are comprehensive and effective.

The organisation must keep a record of all sub-processors that includes the legal name of the processor and the jurisdiction it operates in, and make it available to both the customer and, on request, to supervisory authorities. The Code recommends (but does not mandate) that the list also includes the function of each sub-processor, along with other useful information (which might include the types of data processed, applicable retention schedules, relevant data protection or security certifications, etc.). This requirement is not given an alphanumeric reference in the Controls Catalogue.

Once a customer signs an agreement with the organisation, the organisation must inform the customer that information on engaged sub-processors is available (5.3.E). This information can be provided subject to confidentiality agreements and limited to general information to safeguard processing, though it must at least allow the customer to identify the jurisdictions in which sub-processors operate so that additional safeguards can be applied whenever data is sent outside the EEA.

In particular, 5.3.G requires that, where the organisation has agreed to process the customer's data in certain jurisdictions on the basis of a general authorisation, it must develop a mechanism to notify the customer of any changes to those jurisdictions (e.g. due to a sub-processor moving its data centre).

This part relies heavily on the development and implementation of processes and on the Cloud services agreement itself. The agreement must contain provisions for contract termination, general or specific authorisation in respect of engaging, replacing and terminating sub-processors, and references to specific technical and organisational measures that ensure at least the same level of security as the organisation provides its customers. Confidentiality agreements to allow the provision of information to the customer can be incorporated into the Cloud services agreement or developed as standalone documents.

5.4 International transfers of customer's personal data

This part is preceded by a lengthy disclaimer noting that the EU Cloud Code of Conduct is not considered an approved code of conduct under Article 46(2)(e) of the GDPR (i.e. a code of conduct designed to ensure appropriate safeguards for international transfers). While the Code does contain controls related to international transfers, their broad focus is aimed at ensuring that any transfers performed meet the requirements of the GDPR (and the terms of the Cloud services agreement) without going into the specifics of how that should be achieved.

The organisation remains responsible for ensuring that individual international transfers comply with the GDPR, and the Code explicitly notes that organisations should consider relevant judgements (such as the Schrems II case) and EDPB guidance (in particular, the EDPB's *Recommendations 01/2020 on measures that supplement transfer tools to ensure compliance with the EU level of protection of personal data*) when evaluating transfers.[3]

Control 5.4.A requires the organisation to use the mechanisms provided for by Chapter V of the GDPR when transferring the

---

[3] Organisations should note that transfers of personal data to international organisations in the EEA can be considered an international transfer if the international organisation permits access to the transferred data in regions outside of the EEA.

customer's personal data (i.e. that transfers are made on the basis of adequacy decisions, are subject to appropriate safeguards per Article 46, or make use of an Article 49 derogation), and to ensure that the protective measures provided for in those mechanisms are in place to safeguard individual transfers. While this should already be happening as a matter of course, the organisation should ensure that it has processes in place to evaluate the lawfulness of transfers and be able to demonstrate that the relevant protective mechanisms have been implemented for any given transfer.

Control 5.4.B requires that the organisation only transfers a customer's personal data to a country outside the EEA as agreed with the customer in the Cloud services agreement. This control overlaps significantly with 5.2.D and 5.1.F, both of which relate to ensuring that personal data is only processed in line with the customer's instructions, as defined in the Cloud services agreement.

Control 5.4.C is essentially a duplicate of control 5.4.A, focused on international transfers. It requires the organisation to ensure that transfers of the customer's personal data to a third country (i.e. outside the EEA), as agreed with the customer, meet the requirements of Chapter V of the GDPR. This would naturally be included within the broader scope of 5.4.A (the wording of which applies to all transfers, international or otherwise), so the rationale for its inclusion is unclear, except perhaps to provide a specific data point during audits.

Control 5.4.D requires the organisation to monitor the status of countries to which data is transferred to ensure that they continue to be subject to an adequacy decision. This is most easily achieved by incorporating it into the organisation's process for reviewing relevant legislation and ensuring that records of each review are kept.

Control 5.4.E contains two aspects:

1. The organisation must document the safeguards that are applied to secure each international transfer; and

2. Develop procedures that prevent international transfers from taking place where appropriate safeguards cannot be provided.

The consensus surrounding lawful international transfers under the GDPR is in flux post-Schrems II and is likely to remain so for the foreseeable future, so the procedure should incorporate a mechanism that ensures legal developments in this area are tracked and accounted for (or link to an existing mechanism, if present).

The final control in this part requires organisations based outside the EU but that are in scope of the GDPR (i.e. processes the data of EU residents) to appoint an EU representative in line with Article 27 (5.4.F). This is already a legal obligation under the GDPR, but organisations should expect the specifics of the arrangement to be scrutinised during certification and subsequent audits.

5.5 Right to audit

As required by Article 28(3)(h) of the GDPR, data processors must provide the data controller with all the information needed to demonstrate compliance with the requirements of Article 28 and must allow for and contribute to audits by the data controller or its appointed representative. This part of the Code contains provisions related to these requirements.

The organisation must implement mechanisms to provide the customer with evidence of compliance with both the GDPR and the Code and inform them that such mechanisms exist. Where available, the organisation must provide an executive summary of third-party audits and certification of compliance with the Code (5.5.A). The organisation must also provide the customer with certificates, reports, etc. from third-party audits of the security or data protection measures applicable to the Cloud service (5.5.B). In practice, these will involve certificates and audit reports for the Code itself, and (should the organisation choose to seek certification) for the ISMS mandated by control 6.1.C, alongside any other relevant certifications.

The Code notes that organisations may wish to specify how the requirements of Article 28 are to be met in the Cloud services agreement, and permits the use of a self-service mechanism through which customers may request further information on specific aspects of compliance (e.g. an Internet portal).

The organisation must develop documented procedures that define how customer-requested audits are managed and communicate them to the customer and to auditors, where applicable (5.5.C). It must also provide the customer with the means to request further evidence of compliance with the Code or the GDPR if such evidence is not already available through other means (5.5.D). If not already covered by the Cloud services agreement, the organisation must have in place either additional customer audit provisions, or a procedure that defines how such provisions are drafted when they are needed (5.5.F).

In respect of audit costs, the Code notes that, unless otherwise arranged for in the Cloud services agreement, the customer is responsible for the costs of audit. The Code does state, however, that audit costs defined by the organisation (e.g. employee time spent collating information or assisting an on-site audit) must not be excessive or prohibitive (5.5.E).

5.6 Liability

This part emphasises that the customer must have the right to pursue the liability regime defined in the Cloud services agreement and in Chapter 8 of the GDPR should the organisation act outside the explicit instructions of the customer. The organisation must also ensure that the provisions of the Cloud services agreement do not interfere with the ability of data subjects to enforce their rights. Part 5.6 has only one control requirement (5.6.A), which states that the organisation must ensure it complies with this section of the Code in the event of any dispute with the customer.

Liability regimes should be reviewed by legal personnel to ensure that they comply with the GDPR and any applicable local regulations, and if the organisation has a data protection officer (either in-house, or retained through a third party), they should review the organisation's Cloud services agreement(s) to ensure they do not negatively impact the exercise of data subjects' rights.

5.7 Cooperation with the customer

This part of the Code places requirements on the organisation to assist the customer with data subject access requests (DSARs) and data protection impact assessments (DPIAs), and with the other requirements of Articles 32–36 of the GDPR (in line with Article 28(3)(f)).

The organisation must develop documented procedures that define how it will assist the customer in respect of DSARs (5.7.A). These should address the mechanisms necessary to allow the customer to access and retrieve data, the formats in which data will be provided, transfer mechanisms, and all necessary data protection and information security aspects.

These procedures must be supported by further measures that allow the customer to obtain the information needed to respond to data subject rights requests in a timely manner (5.7.B). The Code states that the customer should be able to retrieve, delete and modify data through the Cloud service itself, or via interactive interfaces or customer portals, and that the organisation should provide reasonable assistance in retrieving, deleting or modifying data (in cases where the data is not accessible to the customer, or cannot be modified or deleted by the customer). This aspect is particularly relevant to the design of new Cloud services, as it is far easier to incorporate these requirements during development than to add them post-release.

As a supplementary measure to the above, the organisation must implement communication channels so that the customer can ask for support with questions and requests in respect of data protection measures and rights requests (5.7.C). Contact forms, email addresses, telephone numbers or any other method of direct communication are acceptable for this purpose, and may be defined in the Cloud services agreement or made available on websites, on customer portals, or via the Cloud service itself. Note that the communication channels should allow contact with both a representative of the organisation and with the organisation's designated data protection point of contact (as described in part 5.9 of the Code).

The next two requirements relate to DPIAs. The first requires the organisation to develop documented procedures that define how it will assist customers with DPIAs (5.7.D). The nature of DPIAs means that the procedure will need to address providing information about sub-processors, the technical and organisational measures used to ensure data protection and information security throughout the processing chain, and certificates, reports, etc. related to compliance with the Code and any other relevant data protection or information security certifications.

Because disclosure to support a DPIA can involve potentially sensitive information, the second DPIA-related requirement (5.7.E) requires the organisation to develop documented procedures that ensure that providing information in response to a DPIA does not create a security risk. To achieve this, the organisation will need to define the information it deems confidential and the reasoning behind that classification. The control notes that information deemed confidential may, to the extent it does not create security risks, be provided subject to confidentiality agreements.

The last requirement in this section (5.7.F) obligates the organisation to communicate information about the processes, time frames, data formats and technical requirements that define how the customer may retrieve the personal data stored in the Cloud service (unless certain conditions are met). The processes and mechanisms used to achieve this should address the deletion of retrieved data where appropriate, in line with the terms of the Cloud services agreement.

5.8 Records of processing

Part 5.8 of the Code contains only two controls, both related to the GDPR's requirements for records of processing (Article 30). 5.8.A of the Code requires the organisation to maintain appropriate records of processing in line with Article 30(2).

1: Data protection requirements

As per Article 30 of the GDPR, records of processing must contain:

- The name and contact details of the controller, any joint controllers, the controller's representative and, where applicable, the data protection officer (DPO);
- The purposes of processing;
- The categories of data subjects and personal data;
- The categories of recipients (including in third countries or international organisations);
- Details of any transfers of personal data to third countries; and
- Where possible, information on time limits for erasure of data and a general description of the technical and organisational measures that safeguard international transfers.

5.8.A also requires that records are kept of all sub-processors that carry out processing on behalf of the Cloud service provider, alongside the above. 'Technical and organisational measures' that safeguard international transfers includes any relevant legal safeguards, such as standard data protection clauses or binding corporate rules.

GDPR-compliant organisations should already have these records in place, but you should consider conducting a review to ensure that all required aspects are present before seeking certification against the Code. Note that, where applicable, the organisation's EU representative must also maintain a copy of these records.

The second control (5.8.B) requires the organisation to develop procedures that enable the customer to provide the information needed to create and maintain the Article 30 records. Organisations may consider incorporating this requirement into existing communications procedures and/or in the Cloud services agreement.

5.9 Data protection point of contact

Like the previous part, 5.9 only contains two controls. The first (5.9.A) requires the organisation to appoint a DPO where required by Article 37 of the GDPR. Organisations must appoint a DPO if they are a public body (except courts acting in their judicial capacity), if their core activities involve carrying out regular or systematic monitoring of data subjects on a large scale, or if their core activities involve processing special category data or criminal offence data on a large scale.

If the organisation is not required to appoint a DPO under Article 37, it must appoint a 'data protection point of contact' that meets the requirements of Articles 37, 38 and 39 of the GDPR (except for Article 38(3) in respect of operational independence). Organisations should pay particular attention to the competency requirements for DPOs defined in Article 37(5), as they are also required for the data protection point of contact.

The second control (5.9.B) obligates the organisation to communicate and make available the contact information for the data protection point of contact to the customer, and to supervisory authorities where required by the GDPR. The information must also be provided to data subjects on request. The contact information must be included in the organisation's declaration of adherence to the Code (and be referred to as 'data protection point of contact'), and the point of contact must remain available for as long as the organisation claims compliance with the Code.

5.10 Rights of the data subject

As defined in Article 15(1) of the GDPR, data subjects may exercise their rights through the data controller, and data processors are obligated by Article 28(3)(e) to help the controller fulfil those rights. Part 5.10 of the Code contains two controls that develop mechanisms to address these requirements.

Control 5.10.A requires the organisation to develop documented procedures that define how data subject requests are handled. The data controller has one month to respond to data subject rights requests (unless the request is complex, or a data subject submits multiple requests), so it is critical that these procedures ensure that requests are communicated to the customer at the earliest opportunity. They should define the communication mechanism, define the roles responsible for communicating (e.g. the data protection point of contact), and provide for verification of the identity of the data subject where appropriate.

The second control (5.10.B) requires the organisation to develop documented procedures that define how the organisation will help customers respond to requests. These procedures should address how the relevant personal information will be accessed (either by the customer or by the organisation), how information will be provided to the customer, the mechanisms through which processing can be restricted or prevented should it become necessary, the mechanisms for modification and erasure of personal data, and any other factors necessary to support the data controller.

Data subject requests received by the organisation may be redirected to the data controller to the extent legally permissible (and assuming that there is enough information in the request to be able to link it to a specific controller). To facilitate this, staff should be trained to recognise the forms data subject requests may take and in how to communicate them to the person responsible for forwarding the request to the controller. The need for timely communication of such requests and the risks of not doing so should be emphasised during such training, and it may be beneficial to repeat this training periodically. It should also be included as part of any employee induction or onboarding process.

5.11 Cooperation with supervisory authorities

All organisations in scope of the GDPR are obliged to cooperate with EU supervisory authorities in respect of their processing of personal data. This part of the Code defines three controls that ensure the organisation is prepared to respond to requests from supervisory authorities.

Control 5.11.A requires the organisation to develop documented procedures that enable the customer to respond to requests from supervisory authorities. Such requests might require the organisation to provide the customer with audit reports, certifications to relevant information security and data protection standards (including the Code), information about information security incidents and data breaches, and descriptions of the nature of the processing and the categories of personal data processed. The procedures should also address how customer communications related to requests from supervisory authorities are identified and prioritised.

The data protection point of contact (or DPO, if appointed) should be responsible for communicating the necessary information to the customer and should be available to support the customer throughout the process. If information is provided through the Cloud service itself, or an associated customer portal or similar mechanism, measures should be taken to ensure that the customer is notified when the information is available.

Control 5.11.B requires the organisation to develop documented procedures that define how it will respond to requests from supervisory authorities. As with the previous control, the procedures should address how requests from supervisory authorities are identified and prioritised, and the roles responsible for communication (in most cases, this will be the data protection point of contact or DPO). The procedures should define the mechanisms through which information (e.g. the Article 30 records of processing) will be provided to the authority in response to a request, including any necessary security measures, and should ensure that responses are provided in a timely and complete manner.

The final control (5.11.C) requires the organisation to develop documented procedures that define how it will notify the customer of requests from a supervisory authority in respect of the customer's personal data, when lawfully permitted to do so. This could sensibly be incorporated into the procedures developed to comply with 5.11.A and B, but should include periodic checks to ensure the legal basis for making such notifications has not changed.

5.12 Confidentiality of the processing

When processing personal data, confidentiality is of the highest importance. The first control in this part of the Code requires the organisation to ensure that all employees, contractors and sub-processors involved in the processing of customer personal data are subject to appropriate confidentiality agreements before engaging in processing activities (5.12.A). Many organisations opt to incorporate data confidentiality requirements into employment contracts; in respect of contractors, some include data confidentiality in the contracts themselves, as a condition of a site-entry permit, or through other mechanisms as appropriate.

Sub-processor confidentiality should be included within processing agreements. This could be incorporated into the processes required by 5.3.C and D, discussed earlier in this book, or defined separately.

The organisation must also ensure that employees and contractors are aware of their responsibilities with respect to confidentiality (5.12.B). This must be achieved using documented policies (e.g. a confidentiality policy) and procedures supported by periodic briefings or staff awareness sessions. For contractors, confidentiality should be discussed as part of a documented site induction or information pack completed when they first attend the premises. The Code's guidance notes that confidentiality policies should "outline the actions to be taken if the employee or contractor disregards the confidentiality obligations", and that the organisation should establish a disciplinary process (if one does not already exist) to manage any disciplinary action that may be necessary.

5.12.C requires the organisation to develop "policies and guidelines" that ensure that data is only processed in line with the customer's instructions, unless the customer explicitly requests otherwise or the processing is necessary to comply with applicable laws or legally binding requests. The guidance for this control, however, does not mention policies or guidelines, instead focusing on "defined processes" that clearly state the customer's instructions, prevent accidental access to customer data, can determine the geographical reach of the processing, and contain a sign-off mechanism for explicit customer requests and exceptions.

While defined processes are undoubtedly more effective in ensuring compliance with the requirements, it may be sensible to ensure that appropriate wording is also included in a relevant policy to ensure that the letter of the control is met.

5.12.D requires that the confidentiality provisions in contracts with employees, sub-processors and contractors must continue to apply beyond the end of the contract. This is standard practice for confidentiality provisions, but all relevant contracts should be reviewed by the organisation's lawyers or legal department to ensure that the confidentiality clauses meet requirements and are lawful.

The next two requirements in this part mandate the organisation to train all employees involved in the processing of customer personal data in the policies and procedures relevant to their role (5.12.E) and data protection more broadly, and to review training and awareness periodically (5.12.F). The latter should be incorporated into the ISMS required by later parts of the Code, for example through competence, awareness or improvement processes.

The last requirement in this part relates to special category data (5.12.G). If the Cloud service is capable of processing special category data (i.e. the Cloud services agreement states that it can), the organisation must have documented procedures to ensure that the technical and organisational measures employed to protect that data can be communicated to the customer, so that the customer can make an informed decision whether to engage the organisation as a processor. The Code also requires the organisation to have regard to member state data protection law in respect of special category data, as some member states place additional conditions on such processing beyond those required under the GDPR.

Due to the potential sensitivity of special category data, the organisation should carefully evaluate whether additional data protection and privacy mechanisms should be employed during processing of such data and implement them where appropriate. In many cases, processing of special category data will require the organisation to conduct a DPIA.

5.13 Assistance with personal data breaches

This part of the Code focuses on the organisation's role in communicating information about data breaches involving customer personal data to the customer. 5.13.A requires the organisation to develop procedures that ensure data breaches are reported to the customer "through appropriate channels without undue delay" and is supported by a requirement that the technical and organisational measures implemented by the organisation must contain "measures that enable the [organisation] to detect, mitigate and report a breach of security".

This latter requirement shares a lot of ground with a subset of the controls defined in Annex A of ISO 27001. A.16 (Information security incident management) contains several controls related to incident management and response, while A.12.4 (Logging and monitoring) contains controls relevant to detection and logging of information security events. If the organisation opts to use ISO 27001 as the basis for its ISMS, compliance with this requirement could be supported by such measures.

5.13.B of the Code requires that the organisation's breach notification obligations and the technical and organisational measures that enable detection, mitigation and reporting of breaches are included in the Cloud services agreement. The Code also states that these measures should address incident management, including planning, detection and reporting, assessment and decision making, responding, and identifying lessons learned at the conclusion of an incident. Organisations that are unsure of the best way to manage information security incidents should consider adopting relevant international standards such as ISO 27035-1 and 27035-2 to support compliance with this requirement.

'Breach obligation notifications' should include time frames for notification of data breaches to affected customers. This part of the Code concludes with a requirement to adhere to those time frames, which necessarily requires that they be defined, though the need for them is not explicitly mentioned in 5.13.A or B.

5.14 Termination of the Cloud services agreement

The final part of the Code's data protection requirements addresses the processes the organisation needs to deal with the customer's personal data after termination of the Cloud services agreement. Per Article 28(3)(g) of the GDPR, the processor must delete or return the customer's data once the contract ends and delete all copies of the data except where required by law.

The first control (5.14.A) requires the organisation to provide capabilities for the customer to retrieve its data "promptly and without hindrance". This refers to specific technical capabilities incorporated into the Cloud service, and the organisation must ensure the customer is made aware of them (e.g. via instructions in the Cloud service itself, or in the Cloud services agreement). The associated guidance notes that, in cases where the personal data is provided by the customer on physical media, the capabilities should ensure that the media is returned to the customer. In such cases, tracked delivery with appropriate insurance (where available) should be used.

The second control (5.14.B) covers much of the same territory, but in respect of the customer's offboarding process at the end of the Cloud services agreement, which may necessarily have to differ from more standard capabilities for retrieval of data. The Controls Catalogue guidance suggests a range of acceptable possibilities, from entirely automated processes to a tiered approach offering the customer multiple retrieval options. ISO 27001 and other ISMS standards contain controls around the transfer of data that may support compliance with 5.14.A and B.

Similar to the GDPR's requirements for providing information to data subjects, the third control (5.14.C) requires the organisation to return the customer's data in a "machine-readable, commonly used, structured format", while the fourth control (5.14.D) requires the organisation to provide information on the format and mechanisms used to provide the customer's data on request.

The final two controls obligate the organisation to delete the customer's personal data within the timescale specified in the Cloud services agreement (i.e. in line with the retention periods defined by 5.2), unless otherwise prevented by laws that require the data to be retained (5.14.E), and to ensure that all storage media that held the customer's data is securely overwritten or otherwise sanitised before reuse or disposal. These requirements should be supported by documented procedures that define the methods used to ensure secure erasure/disposal, and could be linked to ISO 27001 control sets A.8.3 (Media handling) and A.11.2 (Equipment), if the organisation opts to use that standard as the basis for its ISMS.

CHAPTER 2: SECURITY REQUIREMENTS

6.1 General security requirements

All EU organisations involved in the processing of personal data should be aware of the GDPR's requirement to implement "appropriate technical and organisational measures to ensure a level of security appropriate to the risk" (Article 32), and part 6.1 of the Code repeats this requirement.

The first control in this part states that the technical and organisational measures must be appropriate for the sensitivity of the customer's personal data (as much as is possible given the information available to the organisation), as determined by a dedicated data protection assessment (6.1.A). The format of such an assessment is not defined, but should address the suitability of specific technical controls, the potential impact of data breaches, and the 'state of the art'. The latter term sometimes causes confusion, but essentially refers to ensuring that security measures keep pace with technological advancement – if security is rendered ineffective or obsolete by changes in technology or its application (e.g. a new vulnerability is identified in a software platform or mode of encryption), then the organisation must take steps to address the deficiency.

The second control supports the first by requiring the organisation to consider the types and/or sensitivity of the customer's data – to the extent that it has knowledge of them – when assessing the effectiveness of its technical and organisational measures (6.1.B). This can allow the organisation to classify the customer's data according to its sensitivity and provide enhanced security where appropriate, or offer the customer different security options for different types of data or across different services.

Organisations using the Code should also note the requirement in part 6.1 to provide information on available security options for Cloud services to the customer before the Cloud services agreement is finalised (though this will likely occur as a matter of course as the data controller will want to determine the suitability of the service before committing to a contract).

The ISMS

The third control in this part is arguably the most significant and wide-reaching of all those required by the Code. Control 6.1.C requires the organisation to "establish, implement, maintain and continually improve an information security management system (ISMS), in accordance with the requirements of ISO 27001 or any equivalent International Standards".

Of the standards listed in the Controls Catalogue, ISO 27017, 27018 and 27701 are extensions to ISO 27001 and are not considered an ISMS when used in isolation. The remaining standards (NIST SP 800-53, SOC 2, etc.) are presumably equivalent in the eyes of the monitoring body by virtue of their inclusion, though the text of the Code does not directly address the question. If an alternative standard is used, the organisation should consider how it will demonstrate that the controls required by 6.2.A – 6.2.Q have been addressed (which may pose a challenge without a copy of ISO 27001 to serve as a reference).

As many of the security requirements of the Code explicitly reference ISO 27001 controls, ISO 27001 offers the clearest route to compliance with 6.1.C. Regardless of the standard your organisation opts to use, however, this requirement should not be underestimated. Implementing and maintaining an ISMS can be a considerable undertaking, especially in larger organisations, and those that do not already operate such a system would be well advised to start their compliance journey by implementing the ISMS first, then look to integrate the other requirements of the Code once established, to avoid unnecessary duplication of effort.

It is important to note that the Code does not mandate that the organisation certifies its ISMS. Certification involves periodic assessment by an accredited third party to ensure that the ISMS complies with the requirements of the standard. While this inevitably comes with a price tag, it also provides independent verification that the ISMS meets requirements, giving confidence to customers and partners and, in some cases, providing access to tendering opportunities that an uncertified organisation would not be eligible for.

If the cost of certification is not prohibitive (and it should not be in most cases), then organisations should strongly consider it. After all, you will be doing the work whether you seek certification or not, so it makes sense to maximise the potential commercial benefit. Organisations that are implementing an ISMS for the first time should purchase their preferred standard, review the requirements in detail (perhaps with the support of a compliance guide or an experienced consultant[4]) and plan the implementation process carefully to ensure that the project is delivered on time and within budget.

As noted earlier in this book, certification levels two and three of the Code cannot be achieved without independent, third-party certificates and audits of the kind that would result from a certified ISMS. The organisation's desired level of certification under the Code should therefore inform the decision to seek certification for the ISMS.

The final requirement in this part (6.1.D) requires the organisation to justify and document the exclusion of any of the detailed security controls listed in part 6.2 of the Code. Where a control is excluded because an alternative control is already in place, the organisation must be able to provide evidence that the alternative is as effective as the control it replaces.

---

[4] IT Governance Publishing's *Nine Steps to Success – An ISO27001:2013 Implementation Overview, Third edition*: *www.itgovernancepublishing.co.uk/product/nine-steps-to-success*. GRC International Group offers a comprehensive range of consultancy packages to assist organisations looking to implement an ISO 27001-compliant ISMS. For more information, visit: *www.itgovernance.co.uk/iso27001-consultancy*.

Organisations must take care that exclusions from the Code do not adversely affect the operation or conformity of the ISMS. While ISO 27001 allows for controls to be excluded in a similar manner, it requires that security controls are applied on the basis of risk assessment. If your risk assessment indicates that a particular set of security controls are required, then they must be implemented, even if you exclude the security objective in the Code that references those controls.

CHAPTER 3: DETAILED SECURITY OBJECTIVES

Part 6.2 of the Code refers to ISO 27001 "domains" – i.e. the broad categories in Annex A of ISO 27001 that contain specific information security control sets and the individual controls within them.

For example, the 'Human resource security' domain (A.7) contains three control sets:

1. A.7.1 – Prior to employment;
2. A.7.2 – During employment; and
3. A.7.3 – Termination and change of employment.

Within those three control sets there are six individual security controls.

Some of the Code's security objectives require the organisation to implement entire domains, while others are limited to specific control sets within those domains, but the Code uses 'domain' to refer to both. This book will use the terms 'domain', 'control set' and 'controls' accompanied by the reference numbers from ISO 27001, as defined in the example above.

Objective 1 – Management direction for information security

This objective requires the organisation to implement ISO 27001 domain A.5 or its equivalent in other standards. A.5 covers management direction of information security through two controls that cover the development, implementation and review of information security policies.

The organisation will need to demonstrate clear management support for the protection of personal data through management-approved policies covering all relevant areas of information security. This will at minimum include an overarching information security policy that sets out the organisation's commitment to information security and the ISMS, compliance with relevant laws and regulations, relevant goals, etc., alongside other, more specific policies where appropriate. Such policies might include control and use of cryptography, remote working and use of portable devices, data retention, access control, and others as relevant to the organisation and its services. If the organisation implements an ISO 27001-compliant ISMS, several such policies will arise while complying with the Standard.

To be effective, policies must be communicated to employees and reviewed regularly (e.g. annually) to ensure they remain relevant and appropriate to the organisation's goals.

Objective 2 – Organisation of information security

This objective requires the organisation to implement ISO 27001 domain A.6 or its equivalent. A.6 covers the internal organisation of information security and the security of mobile devices and teleworking arrangements.

A.6 contains seven controls, including requirements for defined roles and responsibilities and appropriate segregation of duties with respect to information security, maintenance of contacts with relevant authorities and special interest groups (e.g. EU supervisory authorities, the EDPB), and the inclusion of information security as a key component of project management. While for many organisations this will simply involve formalising existing arrangements (if they are not already formalised), care should be taken in respect of the addition of information security aspects to project management processes. Any existing information security considerations in project management should be reviewed to ensure that they provide effective governance.

To be effective, information security should be addressed not only at the beginning of a project but throughout the process, and consider known and anticipated changes in technology, ongoing maintenance and support of the product or service through its entire lifecycle, and end-of-life aspects such as secure disposal or erasure of stored data.

The final two controls require the development of policies for use of portable devices and remote working, the latter of which must be supported by appropriate security measures to protect data accessed, processed or stored by remote workers. These might include virtual private networks (VPNs), two-factor authentication (2FA) and similar measures, as appropriate for the organisation.

Objective 3 – Human resources security

Objective three requires the organisation to implement two control sets from domain A.7: A.7.1 and A.7.2. These focus on human resource security before and during employment and comprise five separate controls.

A.7.1 focuses on pre-employment screening (which should be proportional to business requirements, including in respect of the sensitivity of data processed) and the inclusion of responsibilities for information security in contracts of employment and those used to engage contractors. A.7.2 contains three controls:

1. Management must require all employees, contractors, etc. to apply information security in accordance with the organisation's policies;
2. Management must provide training and awareness programmes for employees (and contractors, where relevant) in respect of information security; and
3. There must be a formal disciplinary process to take action against employees who commit information security breaches.

Awareness and training programmes should address changes to policies and procedures and the operation of the ISMS, alongside relevant changes in the threat landscape, technologies, etc. Disciplinary processes are likely already in place for most organisations, but they should be reviewed to ensure that they address information security breaches in a sensible manner, recognising that they can occur inadvertently even after the most extensive training.

Objective 4 – Asset management

This objective contains two requirements:

1. Implement domain A.8 or its equivalent; and
2. Control set A.11.2 or its equivalent.

A.8 contains ten controls across three control sets (asset management and responsibility, information classification, and media handling), while A.11.2 contains nine controls covering security of the organisation's equipment.

A.8 covers a lot of ground across its three control sets. The first (A.8.1) contains requirements for inventory and ownership of assets (including information processing facilities), development of rules for the acceptable use of information and assets, and requirements to ensure the return of assets at the end of employment. Asset registers and supporting procedures defining ownership, use and return of assets will assist in meeting this requirement.

A.8.2 requires that information be classified according to its sensitivity (among other factors), and once classified, labelled with the selected classification. Procedures for the handling of assets must also be developed and can likely be combined with the requirement for rules of acceptable use and return of assets in a broad-ranging asset management and handling procedure. A.8.3 covers management of removable media, disposal of media and secure transfer of physical media, and should have its own policy and supporting procedures.

A.11.2 contains requirements for secure siting of equipment, protection of supporting utilities and backup power supplies, secure cabling, effective maintenance, removal of assets, security of off-premises assets, secure disposal and reuse, control of unattended equipment, and clear desk/screen policies. This large list will probably require the development of several procedures and the involvement of multiple departments, depending on the scale of the organisation and the location of its equipment.

Objective 5 – Access controls

This objective requires the organisation to implement domain A.9 or its equivalent. A.9 focuses on control of access to systems and information and contains 14 controls across 4 control sets.

A.9.1 builds a framework for the rest of the domain, requiring development of an access control policy and measures to ensure that employees are only able to access networks and services that they have been authorised to use (sometimes known as the principle of least privilege). The policy will need to address broad requirements for access to systems and information based on the abilities granted by those systems (e.g. admin-level utilities such as PowerShell) and the sensitivity of information (in line with the classification systems developed under A.8.2).

A.9.2's requirements relate to the systems necessary to ensure access control: user registration and deregistration, user access provisioning, management of privileged access rights and secret authentication information (i.e. passwords and other authentication mechanisms), periodic review of access rights, and removal or adjustment of access rights. Given the nature of Cloud services, much of this is likely to already be in place, but the organisation should review each measure to ensure it meets requirements, particularly in respect of periodic reviews and removal or adjustment of access rights, which are often neglected or take place too infrequently to effectively mitigate the risks.

A.9.3 contains a single control: the organisation must ensure that employees adhere to the defined practices for use of passwords and other secret authentication information. Some of these practices will be defined in A.9.4, which contains five requirements for system and application control, including restricted access to information in line with the access control policy, secure logon procedures, password management, additional controls for the use of privileged utilities, and restrictions on access to program source code. Adherence to conditions of use can be incorporated into the organisation's data protection and information security awareness training.

Objective 6 – Encryption

This objective requires the organisation to implement encryption controls for transfers and, where possible, other aspects such as storage, provided doing so is technically feasible and practicable. To comply, the organisation must implement domain A.10 and control set A.13.2 or their equivalents.

A.10 contains only two controls:

1. Development of a policy that defines how the organisation uses cryptographic controls; and
2. A policy on the use and management of cryptographic keys that covers the entire lifecycle.

A.13.2 contains four controls focusing on information transfer, the first of which requires the development of formal policies and procedures defining the organisation's approach to information transfers (which should address use of encryption where appropriate).

The remaining three require that the organisation addresses secure transfer of information in agreements (in this case, in the Cloud services agreement), that information sent via electronic message is adequately protected, and that confidentiality agreements and the requirements that underpin them are regularly reviewed to ensure they remain effective and appropriate to the organisation's needs.

Objective 7 – Physical and environmental security

Objective seven requires the organisation to employ physical and environmental security measures to prevent unauthorised access, deletion or modification of customer personal data, by implementing domain A.11 or its equivalent.

A.11 contains 15 controls across 2 control sets, the first focusing on secure areas (A.11.1) and the second on security of equipment (A.11.2). Note that A.11.2 is already required under objective four, making its inclusion here somewhat redundant – especially so considering that exclusion of asset management while still maintaining a conformant ISMS is a virtual impossibility for an organisation offering Cloud services, which inherently rely on technological assets and equipment.

The six controls of A.11.1 require:

1. Defined physical security perimeters;
2. Appropriate entry controls for secure areas that permit only authorised persons to gain access;
3. Physical security measures for offices, rooms and facilities;
4. Physical protection against natural disasters and other environmental or external threats (e.g. malicious attacks);
5. Development of operating procedures for work performed in secure areas; and
6. Control of areas through which unauthorised persons could enter (such as delivery and loading areas), including isolation of such areas from information processing facilities, where possible.

Objective 8 – Operational security

This objective requires the organisation to take measures to ensure the secure operation of services and facilities involved in the processing of personal data. In particular, the objective highlights the need for backups of customer personal data, and controls on changes to the organisation's facilities or systems that might impact the security of customer personal data. It requires the organisation to implement domain A.12 or its equivalent.

A.12 covers a lot of ground, containing 14 controls across 7 control sets. A.12.1 covers operational procedures and responsibilities, and requires the development of documented operating procedures, a formal change management process, monitoring of resources to ensure adequate capacity is maintained, and segregation of development, testing and operational environments to minimise risks associated with unauthorised access or changes to the operational environment.

A.12.2 contains a single control that requires the organisation to implement appropriate anti-malware controls, including detection, prevention and recovery, supported by appropriate user awareness (i.e. through training). A.12.3 also contains one control, mandating that backups of information, software and system images are taken and tested regularly in line with a backup policy – which means that a backup policy will need to be developed and implemented to define frequency of backups and test regimes.

A.12.4 contains four controls covering event logging and monitoring. Event logs that record user, system administrator and system operator activities, including faults, exceptions and information security events, must be recorded, retained and periodically reviewed. Logging facilities and the associated information must be protected against tampering and unauthorised access, and the clocks of all relevant information processing systems must be synchronised to a single reference source. This latter requirement allows for tracking of events across multiple logs with the necessary degree of accuracy to support investigations.

A.12.5 requires controls on installation of software on operational systems. For most organisations, this will take the form of a 'whitelist' of permitted programs, or a complete prohibition, backed up by technical controls, on the installation of software by anyone other than system administrators.

A.12.6 contains two controls focused on management of technical vulnerabilities. The organisation must seek information about vulnerabilities, evaluate the risk they pose and take steps to mitigate them. It must also develop rules to control the installation of software by users, which will likely tie into the controls required under A.12.5.

Finally, A.12.7 obligates the organisation to ensure that audits, verification activities and similar oversight mechanisms are planned and agreed to minimise their impact on operational systems.

Objective 9 – Communications security

This objective obligates the organisation to secure the transfer of customer personal data across its various systems, networks and processing facilities. It requires the implementation of domain A.13 or its equivalent.

A.13 contains seven controls across two control sets:

1. Network security management (A.13.1); and
2. Information transfer (A.13.2). A.13.2 is also mandated under objective six of the Code (encryption).

A.13.1's three controls require the organisation to manage and control networks to ensure that the information within them is adequately protected; to identify security mechanisms, management requirements and service levels and ensure they are included in network services agreements (including outsourced services); and to segregate information services, users and information systems in appropriate groups across networks (to mitigate risks associated with privilege escalation should an attacker gain access to the organisation's networks).

Objective 10 – System development and maintenance

This objective requires the organisation to ensure that information security is a core aspect of new developments to Cloud service assets (systems, equipment, etc.) used to process customer personal data. It requires the organisation to implement domain A.14 or its equivalent.

A.14 contains 13 controls across 3 control sets. The first contains three requirements related to the security of information systems:

1. That information security requirements are included in requirements for new systems or enhancements to existing systems;

2. That information in application services passing over public networks (i.e. the Internet) is protected from fraudulent activity, contract dispute and unauthorised modification or disclosure; and

3. That information involved in application service transactions is protected to prevent incomplete transmission, misrouting and unauthorised alteration, disclosure, duplication or replay.

The latter two are particularly relevant to Cloud services, as almost all service transactions will take place over the Internet.

The second control set contains nine controls covering security in development and support processes. The organisation must develop a secure development policy and formal system change control procedures, and review and test changes to operating platforms to ensure that security and existing operations are not negatively affected. Modifications to software packages must be discouraged, only made where necessary, and be strictly controlled.

Principles for secure system engineering and secure development must be created and applied across the system implementation and development lifecycle, outsourced development must be monitored, and security testing must be carried out during development. New systems must be subject to acceptance testing, along with upgrades and version changes. The third control set contains only one control related to the data produced by testing, requiring that it is selected carefully, protected, and controlled.

Objective 11 – Suppliers

This objective requires the organisation to protect customer personal data that can be accessed by suppliers or sub-processors. To comply, the organisation must implement domain A.15 or its equivalent.

A.15 contains five controls across two control sets, the first of which (A.15.1) requires the development and implementation of an information security policy for supplier relationships, that information security requirements are established in all agreements with suppliers that have access to, process, store or provide infrastructure components for the organisation's information (including customer personal data), and that agreements with suppliers include specific requirements to address information security risks associated with the supply chain.

The second control set (A.15.2) requires the organisation to monitor, review and audit supplier service delivery on a regular basis, and to manage changes to provision of services by suppliers with regard to the nature of the service, the data involved, etc. This objective may be particularly relevant to Cloud services that rely on third-party infrastructure (data centres, etc.).

Objective 12 – Information security incident management

This objective focuses on managing information security incidents and requires that the organisation implements domain A.16 or its equivalent. It also contains one requirement that addresses something that domain A.16 does not: the organisation must develop documented procedures to establish whether a given information security incident constitutes a data breach. The measures required by A.16 will greatly support those procedures, so it may be sensible to develop the data breach identification procedures after A.16 has been implemented.

A.16 contains seven controls in a single control set. Management procedures must be established to ensure a fast and effective response to incidents, backed up by reporting channels for both information security events and suspected weaknesses or vulnerabilities in the organisation's systems. Information security events must be assessed and classified to determine if they qualify as incidents (and, given the additional requirement of this objective, if they qualify as data breaches).

Incidents, including data breaches, must be responded to in accordance with the management procedures noted earlier, and the information generated by the process of responding to and mitigating incidents must be retained for analysis, with a view to minimising the risk of future events. To support this, procedures that define how evidence is collected and retained must be implemented.

Objective 13 – Information security in business continuity

Business continuity is a critical requirement for many Cloud services, and this objective obligates the organisation to ensure that information security is addressed in business continuity arrangements. It requires the implementation of domain A.17 or its equivalent.

A.17 contains four controls across two control sets. A.17.1 contains three of those controls:

1. The organisation must define its requirements for the continuation of information security during adverse events;
2. Establish documented procedures, controls to ensure the required level of security is maintained during adverse events; and
3. Review those controls regularly to ensure that they remain effective.

A.17.2 contains one control that requires information security facilities to be provided with sufficient redundancy to meet availability requirements. The nature of Cloud services means that availability will probably equate to uptime requirements; these can often be very strict (e.g. 99% or higher), so redundancy measures should be regularly tested to ensure they function properly when they are needed.

CHAPTER 4: TRANSPARENCY

Part 6.3 of the Code requires compliant organisations to be transparent about the technical and organisational measures employed to ensure the security of customers' data. Control 6.3.A obligates the organisation to provide "transparent information" in line with one of the three potential options (called 'demonstration keys') provided. These are:

1. Documents made available to the customer that list the technical and organisational measures taken to address the risks associated with the customer's data;
2. Recent audit reports or certificates of compliance with relevant, recognised international standards (such as ISO 27001); or
3. Verified compliance with the EU Cloud Code of Conduct or other recognised codes of conduct.

Depending on the route the organisation takes to achieve compliance with the Code, at least two 'keys' should be available. Documents can be provided online, or if they contain potentially sensitive information about security systems, could be provided subject to confidentiality agreements. Although it is not stated, 'audit reports' likely refers to independent, third-party audits of a certified ISMS rather than the internal audit reports required by ISO 27001 and similar standards, so the second option may only be available to those that seek certification for their ISMS.

CHAPTER 5: ASSESSMENT AND CERTIFICATION

Initial assessment

Compliance with the Code is monitored by SCOPE Europe. To begin the assessment procedure, organisations must first submit a Declaration of Adherence through a form on the EU Cloud Code of Conduct website.[5] Once a declaration is submitted for the first time, the organisation must download and acknowledge the supporting information provided. The monitoring body will then provide a general set of questions through which the organisation can provide information about the Cloud services it would like to declare compliant.

The monitoring body will assess the information provided against the desired level of certification for each Cloud service. There are three levels of certification under the Code, and the organisation must specify the desired level for each Cloud service as part of the initial assessment (7.6).

Certification levels under the Code relate only to the level of evidence provided during the monitoring body's assessment – the higher the level, the more evidence is required. As a result, higher levels provide greater confidence in the organisation's compliance with the Code, and therefore in its information security and data protection measures.

The three levels and their evidence requirements are as follows:

1. **Level 1** – Internal review and documented evidence of compliance against all applicable requirements.
2. **Level 2** – As level 1, but the documented evidence is partially supported by independent, third-party certificates and audits.

---

[5] *https://eucoc.cloud/en/public-register/declaration-of-adherence/*.

3. **Level 3** – As level 1, but the documented evidence is fully supported by independent, third-party certificates and audits.

Depending on the information the organisation provides, the monitoring body may request further information before deeming a Cloud service compliant, such as samples of records or process documentation, or in the case of organisations with a certified ISMS, audit reports and evaluations conducted by the certification body. Once the monitoring body is satisfied with the outcome of the initial assessment, it will list the Cloud service in the public register.[6]

Each level of certification has an associated compliance mark, which the organisation must use in relevant customer-facing documentation, accompanied by the verification ID assigned to the service by the monitoring body. The mark may only be used once the relevant Cloud service has been declared compliant and listed in the public register, and should act as a link to the register where technically feasible. In cases where the mark cannot be used (e.g. due to technical limitations), a text reference to the Code, containing the verification ID and the web address of the public register, must be provided. Misuse of certification marks may be considered an infringement of the Code.

Ongoing assessment and monitoring

Once a Cloud service is approved for inclusion in the public register, it must undergo annual assessments to ensure ongoing compliance with the requirements of the Code. These are referred to as 'recurring assessments' and must take place at least once every 12 months. Recurring assessments will involve reviews of priority controls, sampling and other measures deemed appropriate by the monitoring body.

---

[6] *https://eucoc.cloud/en/public-register/list-of-adherent-services.html*.

The Code also contains provisions for ad hoc assessments if the Cloud service undergoes significant changes since the previous annual assessment (7.7.1). Such assessments may also occur if a complaint is filed with the monitoring body, or if the body becomes aware of adverse media reports (e.g. news articles about a data breach related to the service) or anonymous feedback that may indicate non-compliance.

Should such events occur, the monitoring body may first request that the organisation takes specific steps to address known issues. The monitoring body will inform the independent complaints panel, which will take action in line with part 7.9 of the Code – actions can include revocation of compliance certificates for one or all services, private formal reprimands, public reprimands and revocation of membership from the General Assembly (a group that provides input into future development of the Code).

If a customer suspects that a Cloud service provider is not complying with the Code, it may submit complaints to the panel, though the Code encourages attempts to find a mutually agreeable solution between both parties before doing so. If a complaint against a Cloud service provider is found to be valid, the provider is liable for the panel's costs involved in the handling of the complaint (7.8.3.3).

Cloud service providers may also submit complaints in respect of any decision made by the monitoring body, in the event that they believe a decision to be unfair or inappropriate.

CHAPTER 6: CONCLUSION

The EU Cloud Code of Conduct has already been adopted by major Cloud service organisations, including:

- Microsoft;
- Oracle;
- Salesforce;
- IBM;
- Google Cloud;
- Dropbox; and
- Alibaba Cloud.

As public and business focus on information security and data protection continues to increase in the face of a constantly changing threat landscape and ever more stringent regulation, the Code offers a visible and independently evaluated way of demonstrating an organisation's commitment to protecting the information it holds.

By requiring compliant organisations to implement an ISMS, it provides a solid foundation of security and data protection controls to support that commitment and aid compliance with the GDPR. Organisations that opt to seek accredited certification for their ISMS will also benefit from further independent evidence of effective security, opening the door to new business opportunities and greater customer trust.

FURTHER READING

IT Governance Publishing (ITGP) is the world's leading publisher for governance and compliance. Our industry-leading pocket guides, books, training resources and toolkits are written by real-world practitioners and thought leaders. They are used globally by audiences of all levels, from students to C-suite executives.

Our high-quality publications cover all IT governance, risk and compliance frameworks and are available in a range of formats. This ensures our customers can access the information they need in the way they need it.

Our other publications about data privacy and Cloud computing include:

- *Data Protection and the Cloud – Are you really managing the risks? Second edition* by Paul Ticher, *www.itgovernancepublishing.co.uk/product/data-protection-and-the-cloud-are-you-really-managing-the-risks*
- *EU General Data Protection Regulation (GDPR) – An implementation and compliance guide, fourth edition* by the IT Governance Privacy Team, *www.itgovernancepublishing.co.uk/product/eu-general-data-protection-regulation-gdpr-an-implementation-and-compliance-guide-fourth-edition*
- *Securing Cloud Services – A pragmatic guide, second edition* by Lee Newcombe, *www.itgovernancepublishing.co.uk/product/securing-cloud-services-a-pragmatic-guide*

For more information on ITGP and branded publishing services, and to view our full list of publications, visit *www.itgovernancepublishing.co.uk*.

To receive regular updates from ITGP, including information on new publications in your area(s) of interest, sign up for our newsletter at
www.itgovernancepublishing.co.uk/topic/newsletter.

Branded publishing

Through our branded publishing service, you can customise ITGP publications with your company's branding.

Find out more at
www.itgovernancepublishing.co.uk/topic/branded-publishing-services.

Related services

ITGP is part of GRC International Group, which offers a comprehensive range of complementary products and services to help organisations meet their objectives.

For a full range of resources on data privacy visit *www.itgovernance.co.uk/data-privacy*.

Training services

The IT Governance training programme is built on our extensive practical experience designing and implementing management systems based on ISO standards, best practice and regulations.

Our courses help attendees develop practical skills and comply with contractual and regulatory requirements. They also support career development via recognised qualifications.

Learn more about our training courses in data privacy and view the full course catalogue at *www.itgovernance.co.uk/training*.

Professional services and consultancy

We are a leading global consultancy of IT governance, risk management and compliance solutions. We advise businesses around the world on their most critical issues and present cost-saving and risk-reducing solutions based on international best practice and frameworks.

We offer a wide range of delivery methods to suit all budgets, timescales and preferred project approaches.

Find out how our consultancy services can help your organisation at *www.itgovernance.co.uk/consulting*.

Industry news

Want to stay up to date with the latest developments and resources in the IT governance and compliance market? Subscribe to our Weekly Round-up newsletter and we will send you mobile-friendly emails with fresh news and features about your preferred areas of interest, as well as unmissable offers and free resources to help you successfully start your projects. *www.itgovernance.co.uk/weekly-round-up*.

EU for product safety is Stephen Evans, The Mill Enterprise Hub, Stagreenan, Drogheda, Co. Louth, A92 CD3D, Ireland. (servicecentre@itgovernance.eu)

www.ingramcontent.com/pod-product-compliance
Lightning Source LLC
Chambersburg PA
CBHW070859070326
40690CB00009B/1907